# Dedications

---

This book is dedicated to all those with disabilities who have constantly been told they can't, only to realize they can.

This book is also dedicated to my mom who taught me to live life with courage, determination, and fearlessness, and who never gave up teaching me how to swim.

The following events in this book are all real life true experiences.

© Copyright 2018 Katie Laurel Wells All rights reserved.

I was born with one arm. I thought God was too tired to finish making me, but then I learned we all have differences, and those differences are the greatest gifts in this world. God makes us all different because that's how special we are.

I learned when I was little that I could still do everything with one arm. I taught myself to use my foot to hold things and open containers. I even taught myself how to paint my finger nails using my foot and how to tie my shoes using my foot as a "helper hand."

When I went to school the other students made fun of me for having one arm. I would cry and cry and cry but then one day I never cried again about this. I decided to be strong and brave. I was always so happy when my mom would pick me up and to go home to my grandpa's rose garden and grandma's graham crackers and milk.

I was thankful when I found some friends who were kind and never once made fun of me. One of them even would hold down the piece of paper for me in art class while I painted. And another friend helped me in computer class with the keyboard when my hand could not reach certain keys.

At my first swim lesson the instructor said I would never be able to swim. My mom searched and searched and found a new instructor who taught me to swim, and not just swim, but swim fast!

Oh, how I soared through the water!

I found freedom in the water and swam so fast I forgot I had one arm. I started competing at many swim competitions.

At one competition this other swimmer laughed at me right before my race and didn't believe I could swim. I finished first place that day in the 50 meter breaststroke.

I was much happier when I switched to the Paralympic swimming division. At those competitions everyone had a disability and I didn't feel different anymore. I even won a silver medal in the 200 meter breaststroke!

I not only loved swimming but also loved to dance. My mom drove me far away to ballet lessons. At the bar exercises I could not hold onto the bar on one side so I learned to balance without holding on.

I even danced in The Nutcracker as a Polichinelle! I loved dance class. No one ever made fun of me or ever asked what happened to my arm. I thought dancers must be the kindest people in the world.

During one Nutcracker performance this beautiful ballerina gave me a pair of her satin toe shoes. She signed them with a blue marker and told me how proud she was of the dancer I had become. I felt proud to know her.

I can still do everything with one arm! I am a champion and so are you!

What is your dream?

The End.

## ABOUT THE AUTHOR

Katie Laurel Wells is a U.S. Paralympic swimmer and has competed both nationally and internationally. She competed at the USA National Championships twice, the World Team Trials, and is the silver medalist in the 200 meter breaststroke at the 2004 Paralympic Swimming Trials. In her free time, Katie advocates for those with disabilities and helps veterans, especially those with limb loss with their recovery. Katie is a Certified Peer Visitor through the Amputee Coalition of America.

**For questions or to book speaking engagements please contact: wells.katie@yahoo.com**
**To read more of Katie's writing please visit: wellslaurel.wordpress.com**

## ABOUT THE ILLUSTRATOR

Frank Carroll is an artist who focuses on exploring the visual and emotional connections between painting and music. The different sounds, and styles of musical creativity affect the way he paints. Frank has a lifelong pursuit of conveying the structure, color, and soul of the music he paints. Using acrylic, foam core, and canvas, his belief is that a song, album, or style of music could be brought to a visual medium, and could be felt and understood. With acrylic, canvas, and layers of acrylic sheeting, he not only is able to set the tone and visual of the painting, but also now adds dimension and depth to the pieces, further delving into bringing a tangible conception to a sonic world.

**To contact Frank or to learn more about his art please visit: frankcarrollartist.com**

Katie and Frank's paths both crossed while working for Blue Ridge Mountain Sports and the two have been lifelong friends ever since.

Made in the USA
Lexington, KY
05 July 2018